Get Clients Today

How to Get a Surge of New, High-Paying Coaching Clients Today and Every Day

Christian Mickelsen

Christian Mickelsen

Christian@CoachesWithClients.com

619-320-8185

San Diego, CA

Limits of Liability and Disclaimer of Warranty

Warning – Disclaimer

ISBN-13: 978-1490997094

ISBN-10: 1490997091

Contents

INTRODUCTION
326 New Paying Clients in Two Weeks

I was inspired to write this book by one of my students, who was able to get 326 new paying clients in two weeks using the strategies and techniques that took me over a decade to develop.

What took me years and years of struggle, study, innovation, testing, and trial and error to figure out, I've been able to share with others to help them get astronomical results way faster and easier than I ever did.

It took me six years to finally become a six-figure coach. However, with the first five coaches that I actually coached, I was able to help four out of five of them get to six figures within eighteen months. And one of them did it within ninety days.

Since then I've helped tens of thousands of coaches get clients and generate a great living doing what they love.

I'm glad you're here, and that you've decided to read this book.

Here's some of what's in this book that will help you get clients and share your blessing with the world...

- A simple three-step process for getting clients

- The three critical success factors for having amazing financial success in your coaching business

- Marketing secrets to get clients faster and easier than ever before

- The "Client Surge" process

- Five ways to get a rush of new clients within seven days

- Powerful "Client Getting Email Templates"

If you wanted to, you could actually take action on just a few ideas from this book and get clients within the next 24 hours.

I'll also share with you some of the Free Session Formula that comes from my program "Free Sessions that Sell: The Client Sign Up System".

A lot of the ideas in this book actually come out of that program. I've jammed this book full with one great idea, after another, after another for getting clients. And of course I'll share the story of my student, Diane, who got 326 new paying clients in two weeks.

Thanks for being a coach, and wanting to make a difference in people's lives.

I hope this book helps. Remember, people need our help. Let's get people coached!

Your Friend & Coach,
Christian Mickelsen

CHAPTER 1
The Most Powerful Force for Change on Earth

I believe that coaching is the most powerful force for change on Earth. Coaching has changed my life a hundred times over. Your work matters. I really want you to be successful. People's lives depend on it. Like mine did 13 years ago...

I got my start in the world of coaching as a client. I was in a job I hated. I was in a relationship that wasn't working. I was out of shape. I had started a business that was going nowhere. But that's not all.

I had this coworker, Charles, harassing me all the time, and publicly humiliating me every day. I didn't know what to do. I just wanted to disappear. I felt stuck. I felt trapped. I hated the job but I needed the money.

When I took the job, I knew I'd hate it but I figured I would only work there for three or four months until I got my business going, and then I'd quit.

The truth is that when I first took that job, I actually felt good about myself. I felt really strong. But after I had been toiling around not taking the actions I knew I needed to take to get my business going, and after being in that negative environment for a while, I got weaker and weaker.

Charles, would call me a "loser" in front of the whole office. But, he didn't mess with me when I first started there. He harassed other people and I thought, "This guy is kind of a jerk," but he never bothered me because I was strong. But eventually as I lost that strength, he was like a shark that could smell blood in the water. He started harassing me, and I became even weaker and more desperate.

Over a year later, I couldn't take it anymore. That's when I hired my first coach, Colleen. During the next nine months, Colleen helped me turn everything around. I got out of that job. I was able to work for myself full-time in my business, got out of that relationship that wasn't working, got myself back in shape. I started dating again. I felt much stronger.

When I hired my coach, I became stronger again. In fact, the harassing went away before I left the company to work for myself because I became stronger on the inside. I attribute that to the power of coaching.

Coaching Changes My Life Again (My Love Life)...

After I ended my relationship, I was single and dating for four years without getting into a serious relationship. I was dating a lot but nothing was sticking. So what did I do? I hired a coach, and four months later, I met Chelsa, the girl of my dreams and now my wife. We've been together for over 8 years now. We're married and we have a little baby girl named Nala who is as cute as a button, and her little sister Zoey was just born a little while ago.

Coaching is the most powerful force for change on Earth. I believe that coaching can help anyone change anything. Your work as a coach matters. Never forget that real people's lives change because of your help.

Getting clients isn't just about making money and dramatically improving your lifestyle, it's really about changing people's lives. Don't ever let a lack of sales and marketing know-how keep you from helping the people who need you.

CHAPTER 2
The Three Critical Success Factors for Financial Prosperity

Why do you coach? Why do we coach? For me, I quit my job and I started a business but I wasn't passionate about it. So even though I was able to make money doing it and work for myself, which was a huge win, I wanted to do something that mattered more. I thought maybe I could be a coach.

When I coached my first client, who I coached for free, I felt like, "Oh, my gosh, this is so fun, I would do this for free all the time." Of course I knew a couple of things. Number one, I knew that I couldn't make a great living if I was coaching everyone for free. I also realized that when people aren't paying money for coaching, they aren't invested in their results.

Clients that I coached for free or for trade or for very low fees got much worse results, or slower results, than clients who paid higher fees and signed up for longer periods of time. In fact, one of my clients totally started taking off after our very first session, not just because of my coaching. Yes, I had one really good session with her. But, I really believe it was because she just stopped procrastinating. She started taking action. **Paying for coaching starts the coaching**.

I don't recommend coaching anyone for free, even if you're just starting out. It's much better to take on clients that are paying, no matter what they're paying. Even if they're not paying very much, they are still more invested. They really want the coaching. They really want to make changes, versus, "All right, I'll let you coach me. But I'm not really motivated to make major changes in my life right now."

We want to coach people who are motivated for change. The truth is there are millions of people who are motivated for change—deeply motivated for change—right now. So instead of just trying to coach anybody, we want to coach the people who are already hungry for change. **Coach the people who want coaching. Coach the people who want change.**

People don't actually buy coaching because they want coaching. People buy coaching because they want results. **People don't pay for coaching; they pay for results.**

Let me tell you the three critical success factors for having a thriving, financially-successful coaching business.

1. **You have to be able to help your clients produce results.**

A lot of coaching schools are well meaning and they have really great coaching techniques, but they're not necessarily tied right to the result that the clients want to produce. A lot of times coaches are doing processes and fill out worksheets and do stuff with clients that are the coaches agenda for what coaching is supposed to be, but isn't the agenda of the client. It's not focused on the kind of results the client wants.

The first critical success factor is you've got to be able to help clients produce results.

Ultimately, it's the client's responsibility to produce those results. It's not our responsibility; it's the client's responsibility. But we need to keep our coaching focused on the results that the client wants. Of course we do the best we can.

I really believe that results are inevitable if people are willing to do the work. If you keep taking action and you keep working on your inner game stuff and you never give up, you will achieve your results. It's just a matter of time.

For some people, things happen really fast. For some, things take a little longer. I mentioned that with my first five clients, four out of five of those clients went from zero to six figures within eighteen months—and one of them did it within ninety days. Why did one do it in ninety days and the others do it within eighteen months? Who knows. Some of it is the skills and background you bring to the table. Some of it is your mindset and confidence. There are a lot of factors that determine how fast results will happen. The skills you bring to the table, your experience—all sorts of things.

The same is true for any client we get. How long will it take for a client to get the result that they hire you for? Who knows. But will they get there? Absolutely, if they're willing to keep doing the work—both the inner work and the outer work. Of course having a coach just speeds that process along.

Coaching keeps them focused, keeps them on track, keeps challenging them, and doesn't let them off the hook or just fall back into their old ways.

If you want to really improve your ability to help clients produce results, I have a program called "Rapid Coaching Academy" that you might be interested in checking out… www.RapidCoachingAcademy.com

Coaching is the most powerful force for change on Earth. Again, there are three critical success factors for having a financially-abundant coaching business...

1. **You've got to be able to help clients produce results.**

2. **You've got to be able to generate coaching leads (AKA: find the people who want change).**

You've got to be able to find the people who already want change, and generate leads of people who raise their hand and say, "Yes, I want help with change." I'll be sharing a lot of ways to generate coaching leads in later chapters.

The third critical success factor is the most important.

3. **You've got to be able to convert those leads into clients.**

You have to have a way to turn those people who want coaching into people who are paying for coaching. You want to do that for them more than for you. The value that they're going to get for changing their life, growing their business or whatever kind of coaching they are hiring you for, this value is much greater than the value of the money that they're going to pay. No matter what you charge, the value is greater, because results are really priceless.

What is it really worth for somebody to turn their child's bad behavior around? If a child is misbehaving and the parent doesn't know what to do, and as a parenting coach you can help them turn their child's bad behavior around, what is that worth? What will the course of the kid's life be like if they keep having bad behavior? What's their destiny going to be?

If you can shift the destiny of the child, what's the value of that? If you can help a parent develop more peace of mind and have less stress, what's the value of that? As a new parent myself, I know the value is very high.

We've got to be able to convert leads into clients. Because if you can't convert leads into clients, you really don't have a coaching business. There are a lot of coaches out there who are doing all sorts of things to generate leads but are not doing anything to turn those leads into clients.

Maybe they're doing sample coaching sessions and maybe they get a client every one out of 20 sample sessions, but that's a really tough way to grow your business.

You might be wondering, "Didn't you mention that you teach people how to do free sessions?" Well, free sessions and sample sessions are totally different things. We'll go into that in a little more depth later on. I'll give you some of the secrets from my Free Sessions that Sell program.

If you can't convert leads into clients, then you don't really have a coaching business. I've had tons of people tell me that they wouldn't even have a coaching business if it wasn't for our trainings. Even if you can generate lots of leads, it's like having this bucket with holes in it where all the rain is coming in but it's all going right back out those holes. Nothing actually gets collected into the bucket.

Now, if you can plug up those holes, then all the rain that gets in the bucket is going to stay in the bucket.

CHAPTER 3
Why We Coach (The Real Reasons...)

Why do we coach? Do we do it for the money? I know that's not what it was for me. The moment I first started coaching, it felt like, "Man, I would do this for free." I love coaching. I love helping people. I've always loved helping people. I was the kind of kid who would rush down to pick up a pencil or eraser that somebody dropped, so I could hand it to them. I just loved being helpful to people.

But why do you coach? Why do you want more clients? Do you want to be able to do what you love? Do you want to make a great living? Often we think about helping people and wanting to do what we love but we don't necessarily think about the financial impact of being able to make a bunch of money doing what we love.

First of all, some people have a job that they don't like. Or maybe it's a job that they like but it's not a passion that they love, like coaching. So what would it mean to you to actually be able to coach full time? What would it mean to you to be able to make enough money to get yourself completely out of debt? Or what would it mean for you to be able to take a much needed extended vacation somewhere fun (whenever you want, where ever you want)? What would it mean for you to be able to make enough money to really contribute to your family and household, to save money for your kids' college tuitions if you have kids, or save money for retirement?

You may never actually want to retire. When you do something you love for a living, you never work a day in your life, so why would you want to retire from something you love? I know I wouldn't. I don't know that

I will ever retire from coaching. Financially, I could retire right now, but I love what I do. I love training; I love coaching; I love teaching; I love helping.

I think that's why we're here. That's why we're both coaches. It's no accident that you're reading this book today. It's no accident that we were brought together. **Our destinies are intertwined.** I'm hopeful that I can really help. My mission is to get the whole world coached.

This is my bigger mission.

Coaching has changed my life. I mentioned a couple of things—getting out of a job I hated, helping me start my own business and work for myself, finding the love of my life and becoming a multimillionaire because of the power of coaching. (Really the power of personal growth combined with the power of coaching.)

I've been on this personal growth path since I was twelve or thirteen years old, when I first started reading self-help, spiritual growth and personal growth books. All of that stuff obviously contributed to my success, but definitely the number one thing is coaching. It is the most powerful force for change on Earth.

Let me give you another tip: have a bigger mission. My mission is to get the world coached. If you're a coach, you might also want to join me on that mission and that's great. I hope all coaches want to join me in that mission, because I know I can't coach the entire world by myself!

But this mission isn't about me. It's really a mission that I'm playing in. I see this as something that the world wants to have happen. This is something that's good for the world. I'm happy to jump in and help out how I can. I think for me the best way to help out is to help other coaches get clients, so more people can experience the miraculous value and power of coaching.

How you can help out and transform your business is to have a bigger mission.

I was working with a client recently and she is a career coach. She wants to help people find the job of their dreams. To help people find their life purpose and the kind of work that they were called to do. We talked about how she wants to grow her business and clients, and I shared with her my bigger vision for what I thought she could do in this world. She could stand for transforming.

Think about it. In the U.S. anyway, it's probably something like 60% to 70% of people who don't like their job. That means maybe 30% of the people like their jobs.

Think about this. If people were doing what they loved to do and what they were meant to do and were operating from their strengths, they would be more effective employees. If we had a whole world full of people doing what they were the best at and people doing what they loved to do, that would be a really awesome world to live in.

I put it to her like this, "You are going to make a huge impact on the world. You are going to change the world in a really powerful way and I'm excited for you." She started connecting herself to a bigger mission. It's not just, "Hey, I'm going to get some clients and I'm going to have a business that I love, a job that I love for myself and make a little bit of money." Now it's a bigger mission that she's on.

I think we can all find a bigger mission to be on. When you have the bigger mission, people are drawn to you. When you have a bigger mission, you're going to be a much more effective marketer, because you're not in it just for yourself. You're not even in it just for your clients. You're in it for the betterment of all humanity. There's a lot at stake here.

CHAPTER 4

The Simple Three-Step Process for Getting Coaching Clients

This is the simple three-step process for getting coaching clients.

Step One: Clients somehow hear about you

Step Two: They have an intro coaching session with you

Step Three: They hire you

First of all, there are a lot of people who aren't doing anything so that people can somehow hear about them. They're not doing any marketing activities. That's a problem. Why is it that people aren't doing those things?

Perhaps they don't know what to do; they don't know where to go or they don't know where to find clients. They might not be sure how to even go out in the world as a coach.

Step two is they have an intro session with you. What do you do in those intro sessions to get people to step three?

If you're doing things so that people somehow hear about you but they're not having an intro session with you, that's a problem. If people are having an intro session with you but they're not signing up for coaching, that's another problem. Those are the two biggest problems that most coaches face and I want to make sure that we solve both of those problems for you.

People somehow hear about you, they have an intro session with you, and they hire you. The great thing about that three-step process is that it's simple. It's not complicated. We often over-complicate our coaching businesses, but it doesn't have to be complicated. It can be very simple. There are a few things that you could do to get people to somehow hear about you. There are things you can do to get people who do hear about you to have an intro session with you.

There are a lot of ways to generate coaching leads, which we're going to get into, and I do have another training program for that called "Client Attraction & Money Making Mastery." It's all about how to generate coaching leads and build your list, where to find clients, where to go out in the world, how to present yourself, how to talk about coaching, how to get clients speaking and networking and all of that. If this is the biggest difficulty for you in your business, you might want to check out that program at www.ClientAttractionAndMoneyMakingMastery.com.

But once you get those leads, how do you get people to have a session with you? One of the things you can do is around packaging your intro sessions.

Let's say you're going to a networking event, you're giving a presentation, you get a chance to give a talk somewhere locally in your area, or are on a teleclass somewhere. Most coaches actually don't even make an offer. They just wait for somebody to think, "Wow, I need a coach and I've heard of Betty and I have her card. Now I'm ready. I'll give her a call." Most coaches are just waiting for the phone to ring.

You are not going to do that. You're going to actually make an offer. You're going to give people something of value, which is an introductory coaching session.

What most coaches do, if they do offer an intro coaching session, is that they just offer a thirty minute no obligation coaching session. That's not very enticing. That doesn't get people to go, "Oh, my gosh, I really want to have a coaching session." The majority of people who take coaches up on those thirty minute coaching sessions oftentimes are other coaches. They think, "Oh, a free thirty minute coaching session.

I'll get some free coaching." Coaches know what the value of coaching is, but prospective clients don't. They often don't understand coaching; they don't understand how coaching works; they don't understand why it's valuable.

We need to talk to clients in their language, and the language of clients is the language of results.

Let's say you're a relationship coach and you work with women who are single to help them find the love of their life. Instead of offering a thirty minute no obligation coaching session, instead offer a thirty minute "Find Your Soul Mate Now" coaching session.

During the session:

- We'll work together to create a crystal-clear vision for the kind of man you'd like to attract and the kind of relationship you'd like to have together.

- You'll uncover hidden challenges that may be sabotaging your success with men and dating.

- And you'll leave the session renewed, reenergized and inspired to finally find the love of your life once and for all.

You see how that offer is a million times more compelling than just a free thirty minute no obligation coaching session? It's clear because we're talking about results.

Are they going to have their soul mate by the time they leave the call? Of course not. But they're going to be started along that path, and those bullet points above are the deliverables that we promised. We're going to help them get crystal-clear on the kind of man they'd like to attract and the kind of relationship they'd like to have, we'll uncover hidden challenges that may be sabotaging their success with men and dating, and they'll leave the session renewed, reenergized and inspired to finally find the love of their life once and for all.

Those are the deliverables. Those are the things we say are going to happen during our free session and those are the things that actually do happen during the free session, at least if you use the Free Session Formula from my Free Sessions that Sell program.

We aren't over-promising. We are just talking about the results that they're looking for. Obviously it's up to them to produce those results. Now, if they hire you, of course then you can help them achieve those results long-term. If they don't hire you, then everybody loses out. They miss out on getting the help that they need.

I went four years of dating without getting into a great relationship. As a result of the coaching I received, I was able to turn things around and get into this amazing relationship I have right now!

CHAPTER 5
How I Cracked the Code

Something I don't normally share is that my previous business was a gift certificate business. This was in the early dot com days right before the dot com bust, and people could order gift certificates from stores and restaurants from my website. Now in grocery stores you can go in and buy gift cards for all sorts of different places, but this was a much newer idea back then.

What a lot of people don't know is that as I was growing my coaching business, I was struggling the first few years. In fact, I fell behind on my mortgage every couple of months. I would catch back up, then fall behind again. This was back ten to twelve years ago before falling behind in your mortgage became so popular! I was really worried about losing the house.

In fact, I was actually worried about losing faith. I was really worried that people would think I was a really unsuccessful coach if I couldn't pay my mortgage and if I lost my house.

In those early days I was actually living off of those gift certificates from the business that I had started. I was still selling some gift cards, but I was putting all my attention into my coaching business. So I had all these gift cards that I bought, which was one reason why I was so in debt. I had to buy these gift cards at a discount so that I could resell them at face value.

So anytime it was somebody's birthday or Christmas or any special occasion, what did they get for a present? A gift card! And guess how I fed myself during some of those days? I would go to the same restaurants all the time. I went to Olive Garden and Red Lobster over and over again, because those were the places to which I had large supplies of gift cards.

Then for business meetings or networking sessions, or when I'd meet somebody for lunch, I would end up paying. Partly this was because I thought it would really impress them if I paid, and I'd look more successful. It was also because I didn't want them to know I was paying my half of the bill with a gift card. I was kind of embarrassed about that.

That's one of my big dumb flaws that I've been working on over the years. I've made a lot of progress but I still have some work to do on always wanting to look successful. It's ridiculous. I still feel this even as a millionaire, now that I have friends who are making more millions than I do! I don't try to pretend I'm making millions more than I do, but I notice that I'm still comparing myself to others, even at this level.

We believe that if we achieve something we'll be happy. I was actually happier making a quarter million a year than making a million a year. I felt more successful then, because I didn't know anybody else making a quarter million a year. Now, even though I'm making millions, I know people who are making more millions. It's something I'm working on. I'm sure there are probably coaches reading this book right now who would volunteer to help me do some more personal growth work on this, so thank you for that! I know I'm not perfect by any stretch.

I mentioned I fell behind on my mortgage a lot back in the early days. It was really tough. It was really, really frustrating. I remember at one point I was taking the garbage out and I was thinking, "Man, I should just throw in the towel and get a regular job. Maybe just get a job as a garbage man where I don't have to think so hard." I was working probably 60-70 hours a week. I was working on weekends. I wasn't with clients; I was just working hard trying to figure out how to get clients, working on marketing materials that didn't really work, working on strategies and all kinds of other things that worked a little bit. I was getting some clients, but I wasn't seeing the results I wanted.

The good thing is that through all of my struggles I was starting to crack the code on how to get clients, until finally I was making a great living in coaching. That's when a handful of coaches sought me out to get my help growing their businesses.

I was able to help four out of five of those coaches go from zero to six figures within 18 months.

And one of them did it within 90 days!

If you're frustrated that your coaching business isn't where you want it to be, just know that everything can change. And the good news is, it can happen fast. It doesn't have to take six years to get to six figures like it did for me. We don't know how long it will take for you, but it's very possible that it can take just a few months.

CHAPTER 6
Make Them Want You

If you want more clients, then I hope you now agree that the gateway to clients hiring you is through an initial consultation, free coaching session or intro session. So it follows that the more potential clients that you can have 1-on-1 consultations with, the more clients you'll get and the more money you'll make.

Plus, with more clients, you'll be doing more of the work you love, and have a lifestyle most people only dream of! Therefore, you need to get more people to want to have a free session with you.

At some point you could be getting too many people wanting to have a free session with you. At this point (or even before this), you may want to start charging for your initial session. There are three benefits to charging for an initial session. The first benefit is that you get paid for your time, instead of giving it away.

Even while you're talking to a client about potentially hiring you, you could be charging for this. The second benefit is that when you are paid for your time, you're perceived as an expert and you are even more likely to get hired by these people. Finally, when you charge for your initial session, you "weed out" people that are just trying to get free stuff from you and you only end up with real, serious, potential clients.

That doesn't mean that I recommend you start charging for your initial session right away. This is because it's harder to get people to pay for that session than it is to get people to take it for free. So, you could end up weeding out potential customers. Some people wouldn't pay for the initial session, but they would become clients.

I think of it in terms of a flood gate. How open do you want your flood gate? If you're fairly new in your business, you probably want your flood gate wide open. Take as many initial sessions as you can get! There are a few reasons why this is a good idea. One is that you probably need practice working with people. Another reason you'll want the flood gate wide open is because having more intro sessions is a way for more people to get to know you.

When you're starting out, you want more people to get to know you and what you do. Later you can start tightening up the flood gate and be more selective about who you let through. You can tighten up by having people fill out a form (online) or fill out a very short questionnaire (via email) to make sure they are good potential clients for you before you have a free intro session with them. Finally, to really tighten up, you can charge people for the session.

Some people ask me, "But is it really hard to give free sessions away?"

In this day and age, *everything* has to be "sold". Even things that are given away for free get rejected all the time! This is because most people can't take the time to interpret and analyze everything that crosses their paths. Think about it. We are on information overload and if we can't find the value in something quickly, we move on.

Think about when you get your mail and you go through it at the garbage or recycling, trying to decide what to throw away and what to keep. If there was a $500 bill in an envelope that looked like one more piece of junk mail, you'd probably throw the envelope away un-opened! That's what happens to most offers for a free intro session.

Most coaches and consultants make a free session offer that makes people have to interpret and analyze the offer to find where the value is for them. What does this do? It makes most people tune out and say things like, "that's nice," but not take you up on your offer.

As I mentioned, many coaches will use something like this: "I offer a free thirty minute exploratory coaching session so we can both decide if working together is a good fit."

How excited are you feeling right now about getting a session like this? You could be falling asleep on me! Let me explain why this doesn't work and keep you from making similar mistakes. Let's go deeper into the offer than we did in Chapter Four.

The example above doesn't work because you don't immediately see what you're going to get out of having a free thirty minute session. All you see is two things. First, that it's going to take up thirty minutes of your time. And second, that this session is about hiring someone, which is scary because it's probably expensive! Maybe you don't really even know if you're anywhere near close enough to hiring a coach (if you even know what one is or does) to take this big of a step.

There are three things you can do to beef up your introductory session offer to make it ten times more compelling. First, give your session a concrete and compelling name. Second, create a list of powerful outcomes or results that people will leave your session with that they didn't before. Third, create perceived scarcity.

Let's start with the name. The idea behind giving your introductory session a name is that your potential clients will be able to immediately put their arms around the benefits they'll get from the session. They'll understand what the session will do for them.

Use your creativity to generate some powerful, compelling names for your initial session. For example, if you are a relationship coach, call your session, a "Relationship Rehab Coaching Session", or how about...

The first 5 people to respond to this email will get a free 25 min. "Find Your Soul-Mate Now" 1-on-1 coaching session with relationship expert [your name here].

Or if you're a business coach: Get your free 25 min. "Explosive Business Growth" 1-on-1 business consultation.

Does this make sense?

Here are some of the elements of a great name.

- It is focused on something people already want (like love, money, happiness) or…

- It is focused on eliminating something they don't want ("Erasing Overwhelm" Coaching Session).

- It is clear, concrete, and specific.

- It is short (2-5 words max.)

What names can you come up with for the work you do?

Note: Even if you're not a coach, but perhaps you're a financial planner or some other type of expert or consultant, you can call your session a "coaching session".

Once you have named your session, the next thing you'll want to do is create some powerful expectations for what will happen in your session. You need to let them know what good will come of investing their precious time!

For example...

Get your free 25 min. "Relationship Rehab" Coaching Session 1-on-1 with [your name here].

In this powerful session you will leave with:

- Written positive outcomes for your relationship

- A new awareness of what is causing many of the challenges in your relationship right now (they may not be what you think!)

- A renewed sense of energy about turning your relationship around (or you'll know if it's time to call it quits)

- A "next-step" action plan for moving your relationship into the next phase of love, connection, and passion!

Can you see how much better this is?

Here are the elements of positive expectation statements.

1. They are real actual things people will take away from your free session (of course you are not just making these things up).

2. They contain very specific tangible things (like "written goals").

3. They contain very specific intangible things (like "renewed energy and motivation").

4. They relate to what you do (i.e. if you are a business consultant "renewed energy for your business").

Do you think you could come up with a list of powerful expectations that people will get from your initial session? Give it a try, right now!

Note: I teach people to conduct initial sessions in such a way that it creates tremendous value for the potential client, and motivates them to hire you. This process is called "Free Sessions That Sell: The Client Enrollment System". If you don't know what benefits people will get from having a session with you, or if you don't have a great way of delivering value and motivating people to hire you at the same time, then I recommend considering the purchase of this program. Go to www.FreeSessionsThatSell.com to check it out.

The last thing you'll want to do to make people go crazy for your initial session is to frame your offer. When we can have something anytime we want, we don't seem to value it as much. But, if it is rare or scarce, we go crazy for it. Back in the early 90's I was really into comic book collecting. In the comic book store, whenever I saw an issue was close to selling out, I thought about buying it because I thought it was rare and might go up in value quickly. It was an illusion because they often had another big stack in the back room! Have you ever been motivated to get something because you thought you might miss out on it if you didn't get it now? Me too! I think we all have.

It's good to frame your intro session offer in such a way as to make it seem even more valuable. Before I explain how to do this, I want you to think about how many intro sessions you'd like to have each month. Ten? Twenty? Thirty? You might say, "I'll take as many as I can get!" and that makes sense. But, if you had twenty per month, that would be four potential client meetings each week. If you have that, you'll grow your business pretty fast! So why not set a limit on the availability of your free sessions. The truth is you can't do a thousand free sessions in one month, so why not limit yourself and let people know that there are limits.

Here are some examples:

1. This offer is available to only the first 5 people to respond to this email.

2. If you would like to have one of these free sessions with me, please reply and I will pick 5 winners at random from all of the people who respond.

3. This session is normally $197, but as a gesture of goodwill to my audience, I'm making it available for free to the next 10 people only! I only have 10 spaces open for these sessions all month and once they are gone, they're gone!

I think you get the idea. The key here is to be as real as you can about this. Of course you don't want to lie. You just want to frame the truth in a way that makes you and your coaching even more valuable.

If you're sitting around in your pajamas all day doing nothing because you only have two clients (and one of them is a barter deal), you don't want to project this kind of image to the world. It may be true, but you'll be more attractive to clients if you can frame yourself and your initial session offer in a way that is compelling from start to finish. Agreed?

Note: You can create several intro session offers. Simply take the basic offer that you've come up with and spin it in a different way. Then you'll keep your offers fresh. For example you could offer a "passion into profits" coaching session and a "business start-up" coaching session and an "explosive business growth" session.

What you do with people during the session could be the exact same thing, but the way you describe it might be slightly different. Each offer could appeal to different people. By switching up your offers, you'll be able to reach more people and keep your offer appearing rare and valuable.

Here's a quick re-cap:

1. The way to get clients is to offer a free initial/intro session and then convert them into ongoing, paying clients.

2. If you want to get more clients, one key is to create an enticing initial session offer.

3. There are 3 things to put into your initial session offer.

    A. A powerful and compelling name for your session.

    B. A list of positive expectations/what people should expect to happen in their session with you.

    C. A "frame" for your offer that makes the offer seem even more valuable.

CHAPTER 7
Five Ways to Create a "Client Surge" On Demand

Let me tell you about some ways to get a rush of high-paying clients this week.

First, if you want to have a client surge, you need to create that client surge e-mail, the client-getting e-mail or client-getting offer. You want to have that really good, red hot, free session offer for your coaching. (If you haven't already, check out the Client Getting Email Templates at the back of this book!)

I'm calling it your client-getting e-mail, but you can use it in all sorts of different ways. There are actually five great ways to get a rush of new high-paying clients. Number one is if you have an e-mail list you could send it as an intro session offer to your list and get a rush of people wanting to have a session with you right away. Then the only thing you need to do is know how to have a great intro session.

There are probably people reading this book who already are able to sign up clients from their intro sessions, but you want to learn how to sign up a higher percentage of people. If you're signing up two out of ten clients right now, I want you to learn how to sign up four out of ten, five out of ten, nine out of ten—even, essentially, ten out of ten clients that you have an intro session with could end up hiring you.

I've had many students of mine go ten for ten, fifteen for fifteen. I don't know what the record is for most consecutive clients signed up from intro sessions. Maybe that should be a contest - to see who can get the most consecutive intro sessions with people signing up! Although, of course it's not about that. We don't want to force an outcome. We don't want to try to force these signups.

The truth is that nobody is going to get 100% all the time. For most coaches, what you need to learn is how to sign up a higher percentage of clients, more consistently, at higher fees.

#1: Create a "Client Surge" With Your Email List

You want to take that client-getting e-mail or that free session offer and you want to send it out to your e-mail list. That one action alone could get you a rush of people wanting to have an intro session with you. You could get ten people, twenty people, one hundred people—or even hundreds of people—to want to have an intro session with you depending on the size of your e-mail list.

You might be thinking, "I don't have an e-mail list. What do I do?" If that's the case you could actually send it out to your friends and family and just say, "Hey, here's this cool thing I've got going on right now and it's free. It might not be for you." You might say, "I help women find the love of their life," and you might send it out to your male friends. You could just say, "Hey, guys, if you have any single female friends, please forward this on to them," and you could get some sessions lined up.

#2: Create a "Client Surge" At Networking Events

One way to get a rush of clients is to send out your free session offer to your e-mail list. A second way to get a rush of new high-paying clients is to go to live in-person networking events and give a 30-second commercial. A lot of times when you go to networking events they let everybody give an introduction to the whole group and you get to give what's called a 30-second commercial. Sometimes they let you do a 60-second commercial.

What you want to do is quickly introduce yourself. Say, "Hi, my name is Karen and I'm a relationship coach. And because I'm new to the group (or because I've been a member of the group for a year—or whatever reason) I'm offering a special 30-minute Find Your Soul Mate Now coaching session. During this session, we're going to create a crystal clear vision for the kind of person you'd like to date." Basically go through the client-getting free session offer. Just tell people, "If you're interested in having this special session with me, make sure I get your card when everyone's done with their 30-second commercial and I'll have someone from my team contact you to set up your session."

You could say someone from your team—and it could be you. But you could also get somebody else to call and schedule those appointments, too. I myself have done this strategy and I've gotten eight or so people from a 30-second commercial want to give me their card to get a session. Some of my other students have had as many as fifteen people want to have a free session with them.

You could do this at a networking event and get a rush of high-paying clients. Let's say you get fifteen people who want to have an intro session with you. If you sign up ten of those people as clients, that might be enough to get you from zero to six figures. I don't know if you even want to get to six figures, maybe you have an entirely different goal for your coaching business.

Go where your clients are. Network where your clients are. Going to a networking event with lots of coaches in it might not be the best idea, because for most people, coaches aren't your target market. It's not really a great place to hang out. It can be helpful. I'm not saying don't go to any meetings where there are other coaches, but if you're a business coach, go where business owners are hanging out. If you're a relationship coach, go where people looking for relationships might be hanging out. Go to a seminar on relationships and network and hang out with the other people in the audience letting them know that you're a relationship coach and you're there to learn more tips from the speaker so that you can help your clients even more.

You could tell them that In the meantime, if they want some one-on-one help they could get a free session with you - since you just met them and you'd like to help them out. Invite them to have a free coaching session with you. Network where your clients are.

#3: Create a "Client Surge" With Partners

You can also partner with someone. Let's say you are a relationship coach. Partner with a single's meet up group, singles mixers or speed dating group. Maybe you could actually do a training for them—some public speaking. Or even invite them to send out a free session offer for you to all their people as a value-add for anybody who signs up to go to their next event.

Partner with somebody and get a partner to send out a free session offer for you. That is a hot way to get clients. Some of my students have done that with amazing success. In fact, one of my students got twenty new clients in thirty days. His name is Mamoon and he coaches people on the Quran.

If you can get a joint venture partner (somebody who works with your same target market) to send out an intro coaching session for you, you can potentially fill up your whole business.

All of these little strategies in and of themselves could be ways to fill up your whole business. If you do all of them consistently, you could always have a full coaching business and you can make more than $100,000 a year. You could make a quarter of a million dollars a year. You could make millions of dollars a year using these strategies. You could make as much money as you choose and help a whole lot of people.

#4: Create a "Client Surge" From Public Speaking (Or A Book)

Another way to get a rush of intro sessions is public speaking. If you get a chance to give a talk or do some public speaking, you can do your training and at the end of your talk you can offer an intro coaching session. If you have fifty people in the audience and you give a really hot offer for a free coaching session, between 80 and 100% of those people are going to want to have a session with you. Assuming you're a decent speaker and you've shared some great techniques, people would want to get your help.

I would imagine if I were teaching the information in the book at an event and offered an intro session to everyone in the room, a free "Zero

To Six Figures In Your Coaching Business" session and told you that during the session we're going to:

- Create a crystal clear vision for ultimate success in your coaching business

- Uncover hidden challenges that are keeping you from getting all the clients that you want and more, and

- You'll leave the session renewed, reenergized and inspired to create the coaching business of your dreams once and for all

If I offered something like that to everyone at the event, I have a feeling there would be a lot of people who would be interested in signing up just based on that fact that I've been sharing a lot of great tips for getting clients.

#5: Create a "Client Surge" From Social Media

This one is pretty simple. Post your red hot free session offer on your website or blog and then send out tweets or FB status updates letting people know about your super special offer.

For example you could tweet...

"I will personally help you find your soul mate for FREE. Click here for details www.whateveryourwebsitenameis.com

OR...

"Trying to lose weight? I will personally help you lose it all and keep it off forever. Get 1-on-1 private coaching w/me FREE ---> *www.shortendurl.com"*

OR...

"I'll personally help you sell way more and double your commission checks w/totally FREE 1-1 coaching with me. Details on my site ---> *mydotcomdotcom.com*

Ok, so we've covered getting clients via...

- e-mail

- networking events

- joint venture partners

- public speaking

- social media sites

Let me tell you one more way that one of my students used. She got 326 new clients in two weeks! How did she do it?

Bonus #6: Create a "Client Surge" From Social Deals Sites

You've probably heard of Groupon. Groupon is basically a group buying website. With Groupon, they have a special deal. Usually it's 50% off or 70% off of something, but in order to get the deal to work, enough people have to order it. So if you want the deal, then what you do is you tell other people about the deal and more and more people buy the deal.

What one of my students did is this. She didn't have a niche as a coach and she heard me say, "If you don't have a niche, date a niche. Pick a niche and just see how it goes coaching some people and marketing yourself in that way. Then if it's working for you, stick with it. If not, you can always try a different one."

She took my client-getting e-mail, with the career coaching free session offers—and she partnered with one of these websites that's like Groupon. She's based in Australia and it wasn't Groupon, but it was a similar kind of website. There are more than fifty copycats of Groupon out there, and new ones are popping up all the time!

She partnered with one of them, they ran her offer and she got 326 new clients. These weren't free sessions. She was charging $19 for these sessions. The Groupon type company kept half of that and she got half of that. But here she got 326 people paying for an intro coaching session!

Out of those 326 paying clients who were paying for that intro session, she was getting high 60s, nearly 70%, of those people signing up for one-on-one or group coaching with her. I don't know ultimately what her total number ended up being of long-term paying clients. She may even be still doing some of those intro sessions with people today. That's a lot of intro sessions to do!

You can see how she's got enough clients to last her for a long, long time just from using one strategy.

CHAPTER 8
Adding $100,000 in New Clients Is Easy

There's all this talk about money and making money from your coaching. The truth is, I grew up on food stamps and special lunch programs. As I wrote about earlier, I have this weird drive I'm working through to always seem successful. In fact, that's why I was so worried about losing my house in the early days of running my coaching business. It wasn't actually because I was going to lose my house. It was because then I would seem like I wasn't successful.

I was teased as a kid for basically wearing clothes that were ten years out of style. My older brothers were nine and ten years older than I was, and because we were pretty poor I was wearing the jeans and clothes that they were wearing when they were kids. I was wearing bellbottoms during the 80s. Not very cool.

If I'd had a lot more confidence, maybe I could've turned it into, "Hey, this is so cool." But I didn't. I was very shy, and pretty darn insecure as a kid. For me, feeling like I was poor basically made me feel like I wasn't as worthy as other people. That's a big drive to make money. Partly it's the self-esteem thing.

That said, if that was my only drive for making a bunch of money, I'm grateful that it motivated me to become really wealthy. I went from being $72,000 in debt to being a millionaire. I went from food stamps and special lunch programs for myself as a kid to now being able to basically buy my kids anything. It's not that my daughters want much; my two year old wants to play with rocks, she wants to chase after dogs. It's not like they need a lot.

It feels good for me to know that I can basically take care of my daughters with whatever they want—college, cars, travel. It's not that I want to spoil them either, because certainly having grown up poor, I think it also helped me appreciate things and made me willing to work really hard.

I don't know why you want to make six figures, or make seven figures, make a million, or make ten million or whatever you want to make. But if you want to make six figures in coaching, or a lot more, I want you to know that it's very possible.

$500 a month is really the least amount I recommend coaches start off charging. You could actually take clients on for less than $500 a month, but I recommend having that be your starting point—even if you're just starting out.

If people can't afford $500 a month, you could take the special techniques from my Free Sessions that Sell program. When they tell you they can't afford it, you could say, "What would work for you?" If they say, "I could do $250 a month," if you're a new coach starting out, I would say go for it. Take it. Get more clients and get more success stories, get more experience and get more money coming in.

Even at $250 a month, for four 30-minute sessions if that's what you offer, that's still $125 an hour which is not bad. Now, at $500 a month, then you're getting $250 an hour if you do four 30-minute sessions a month.

So I would recommend charging at least $500 a month. **At $500 per month, you only need 17 clients to make $100,000 a year.**

If you charge more than $500 a month, it gets even better. **If you charge $1,000 a month, then you only need nine clients to make $100,000 a year.** Actually, 8.5 clients makes $100,000 a year. You don't need everybody in the world to become your client; you only need eight clients. And if you charge $1600 a month…

I wrote earlier that one of my clients went from zero to six figures in 90 days. He actually started off charging $1500 a month. I thought, "What are you doing charging $1500 a month?" He was only paying me $700 a month at the time, and I thought it was a bit crazy to charge that much per month, but I didn't say that to him!

I thought, "Wow, if he has the confidence to charge $1500 a month, then he should go for it. Let's see what happens." He actually got six new clients in his first 90 days. He went from zero to six figures in 90 days. The first 60 days he was really just trying to figure things out. He really got six of those clients in one month from doing one of the strategies I wrote about in the last chapter.

You only need between 6 and 17 clients to make $100,000 a year. Again, I don't know if you want to make $100,000 a year. But if you do want to get more clients and make more money then I hope you're going to implement the ideas I'm sharing with you in this book, because these are the keys to making a great living as a coach, and helping a lot of people.

CHAPTER 9
How to Sign Up Clients on the Spot

I mentioned I was going to teach you the three critical success factors for getting coaching clients. They are:

1. You need to be able to help your clients produce results

2. You need to be able to generate coaching leads

3. You need to be able to convert the leads into clients

In the earlier chapters I shared with you many ways that you can generate coaching leads. If you want to learn more about generating coaching leads, I have a program called "Client Attraction & Money Making Mastery" that you might be interested in checking out.

(see www.ClientAttractionAndMoneyMakingMastery.com)

But now let's talk about how you convert those potential clients into paying clients. How do you turn them into paying clients?

You want to avoid a lot of the mistakes I used to make. What I used to do when I first started out as a coach was sample coaching sessions. I actually got clients from doing sample coaching sessions, but when I started out as a coach, I started out charging $195 a month.

Sample sessions can get people to sign up for coaching if the fees are pretty low, but it also took me lots and lots of "sample" coaching sessions to get very few clients. I had to do something like 38 coaching sessions to get six low-paying clients. That's still not too bad. Six clients paying $195 a month is around $1200 a month, and I was actually able to get those clients in my very first month as a coach. I did two talks, two speeches basically, and I was able to get a bunch of people from the audiences to want to have a session with me.

I didn't know everything back then that I know now. I didn't start off charging $500 a month. I didn't know how to sign up clients during intro sessions the way I do now, and I didn't know how to get a rush of people from my audience to want to have a session with me. Obviously I got some people, but not 80-90% the way that we would if I had a really red hot free session offer like I do now.

So how do you get people to sign up for coaching? What do you do during the free session? At this point you know that you don't want to just do sample sessions in coaching. I'll tell you, I didn't know what to do during my intro sessions at first. I knew that somehow I was supposed to get people to sign up for coaching during those intro sessions, but I didn't know how to do that. And when I listened to some trainings on things that people said to do, I thought it was crazy!

I used to do the "Wheel of Life." I don't know if you're familiar with that. You create a circle and chop it up into a pie. You've got relationship, career and all these different things and you have people rate themselves in these different areas on a scale of 0-10. It shows them, basically, where their life isn't great. What I used to do is say, "Pick whichever area you want and we'll do some coaching on it."

What's interesting is they didn't always pick the lowest area. Sometimes they would pick several areas. Like I said, I would get some clients every now and again to pay me my very low coaching fee of $195 a month. But I didn't know how to actually even talk about the money or talk about the coaching fees or actually ask for them to sign up for coaching. I felt really uncomfortable. I felt really weird about money; I felt really weird about asking them to sign up. I didn't want to be pushy; I didn't want to be salesy. I didn't want them to think that I was just there to try to sell them stuff. I didn't know what to do.

I've done so many intro sessions over the years, and I had to try so many different things to find what worked. But that's actually how I developed the Free Sessions that Sell formula. I remember at one time I just did a sample session and I thought I won't even bring anything up about my coaching; I'll just wait until they bring it up. I would just hope they would bring it up and say, "Well, how does your coaching work? How much do you charge?"

I tried that for a while. I probably did five sessions that way, just because I felt so uncomfortable bringing it up. Some people in the session wouldn't even bring it up either. They would say something like, "All right, thank you. This was great." Then they would leave. Some people would ask about my coaching and fees, and then say something like, "Thanks so much for the info. I'll keep you in mind for the next time I feel like I need some coaching."

I tried so many different things. Some things would work and some things wouldn't work. Some things would work well; some things wouldn't work so well. Eventually I cracked the code and I developed a way to really structure the whole intro session in a way that provides tremendous value for the potential clients so they feel like they've gotten so much out of it.

In fact, with this new Free Sessions that Sell process, people get more value than they got when I would just do a sample session. **In any one given sample session, you're usually just micro-focusing on one problem or one goal, whereas in Free Sessions that Sell process, we actually zoom out and look at what it is that people ultimately want to achieve and all the things that are standing in the way.**

It's kind of like creating a road map for them to see exactly what they want and exactly what they need to do, and what's going on that's keeping them from getting what they want.

Then when I talked about coaching, it helped them see how the work that we do as coaches can help them get what they want in their life and help them overcome their challenges. I also developed a way to talk about the fees that feels really soft, very comfortable, very non-salesy.

I never wanted to feel like a salesperson. My brother was a really slick salesperson back in the day and he was just so pushy, and oftentimes manipulative. Ugh. I just felt uncomfortable with that. I didn't want to be like that. I applaud him for his boldness and tenacity, but that's just not something I was comfortable with.

So I developed a way to actually sign up a high percentage of clients at very high fees. Again, you don't have to charge high fees, but you can choose to charge high fees. A lot of times, it's better for the client. The more clients pay, the more invested they are. The more invested they are, the more likely they are to get results. The more likely they are to do whatever it takes to get results.

I want to share from my Free Sessions that Sell program one of these magic phrases that make it very soft and very easy for you to move people closer into working with you without it being pushy or salesy. In fact, the whole process is really a coaching process.

You're not actually trying to get them to buy coaching. You're actually trying to get them the support they need with the goals that they have. You're trying to get them the support they need to overcome their challenges. You're really helping them to make a decision to hire you or not hire you based on what's best for them, without being attached to whether they hire you or not.

It doesn't really matter whether any given client hires you or not. In fact, my philosophy is I want clients to hire me far more for what it will do for them than what it will do for me. I know my coaching is going to change their life. I want them to get the coaching because it's going to be so good for them, not because I'm going to make a bunch of money. Now, the money is great too and important for being able to continue to run your coaching business. But I found that having that approach makes you more money and gives you far greater happiness than having the approach "I want to get money from somebody."

I don't want to get money from people, I want to give them the value. An exchange of value back and forth is really what makes the world go round.

One of my other problems in the early days was just my whole mindset about money and my mindset about coaching. I just felt like, "Man, I wish I could just go help people. I just want to go help people and have them give me money in return. I don't want to have to figure out how to market and sell coaching. In fact, I wish the world would be that way. I wish the world would be set up that I could just go give, give, give, give and the world would just give back to me."

In some ways, it's true. But in other ways, it's not. If I hadn't learned to market and sell coaching, I wouldn't have been able to provide as much value just out there coaching people for free. The value of coaching isn't just in doing the coaching, the value of coaching is in the result. I learned how to structure my marketing in a way that talks about results. I also learned that when people pay for results, they're more likely to get results.

I had to actually work through a lot of inner game stuff about money in order to crack the code and become more successful as a coach. I had to let go of the idea that God got it wrong and he should've set it up so that good-hearted nice people who really just want to help people could just go out and help people and somehow money would show up in their bank account.

I had to realize that I had to work within the system the way the universe was set up. I had to trust that God got it right, that the universe is set up right, that this is the way it's supposed to be. That I need to operate within the system in a way that actually is in high integrity, that feels really good and is very helpful. That's really how I developed the Free Sessions that Sell process.

Let me share a magic phrase with you. You can see how it just makes people really comfortable and connected. During free sessions with people, they never feel like I'm trying to sell them; they only feel like I'm trying to help them, like I'm already their coach.

One of the magic phrases is: **"I have a program designed specifically to help people overcome these sorts of challenges that you mentioned and achieve these kinds of results that you're looking for. Would you like to hear a little bit about it?"**

It really feels good. Would you like to hear a little bit about it? Certainly if they said no, then we could wrap up the coaching session right there. Of course 99% of the time they say, "Yes, I'd love to hear about it." In fact, it's a breath of fresh air for them. They feel like, "You have something that could actually help me?? Please tell me. I have these problems. I do need help."

If you're reading this book and you have trouble signing up clients, then hearing about my program "Free Sessions that Sell," could give you a breath of fresh air. "Oh, my gosh, you're going to actually tell me how I can sign up clients in a way that's really comfortable? I can actually sign up a high percentage of clients? I can actually get clients that pay a really good investment for their coaching? I can make a great living as a coach? I don't have to struggle anymore, and I don't have to keep striking out in my intro sessions? I don't have to keep going away and figuring how to even get people to have intro sessions with me? You're going to actually solve this problem for me?" It's a breath of fresh air to hear how something can solve your problems and help you achieve your goals.

So that's one of the magic phrases, and here's one more idea for you.

Hot Secret For Signing Up Clients...

A little secret I learned a while ago was that if you have a contract to be filled out, have the client fill it out instead of you. This is because as they're writing, every letter they write on that contract (name, phone number, etc.) is a reinforcement that they really want to go for it and do this. That they really want to sign up for the coaching. It's not a big deal. It's just one little thing to do if you are having sessions in person with people.

You actually have more power to influence people in person, so if you're just starting out, do your sessions in person if you can. But as you get more and more busy, definitely do them over the phone because it's much more convenient time-wise to just have phone sessions.

Guarantee Your Coaching...

Another big idea is to guarantee your coaching. A lot of coaches are afraid to guarantee their coaching. In the Free Sessions that Sell program, I have specific language for how to guarantee it, but ultimately when you guarantee your program, it makes people feel safer to try it out.

Most people want to hire you but they're a little afraid. They might be thinking that they don't know if coaching is going to get them the results they want. That even if you are a great coach, they may not be a good client. That it won't "work" for them. So if you offer them a 30-day guarantee, it gives them a chance to try it out for 30 days and it makes it so much easier for people to say yes.

Let me tell you my results with it. I've been offering a guarantee on my one-on-one coaching for years and I've only had two people ever take me up on it in all the time that I've been coaching. It's very unlikely. The risk on your part is very low to offer the guarantee, but the rewards are so great because it makes it so much easier for people to say yes and hire you.

I'd like to give you more background on how I developed the Free Sessions That Sell system.

I started out like most coaches only with one BIG exception. I had sales training. But, even though I had great sales training and tons of successful sales experience, I didn't apply it to coaching. You see, for me coaching was this special "heart centered" thing you did from a loving place and "selling" had little to do with coaching.

I did the same things most coaches do: I coached my heart out trying to "hit a grand slam home run" by solving all of my potential clients problems in one "superman" free coaching session.

I did free session after free session with the same mediocre results. Few people hired me. I actually got lucky and picked up a handful of clients because of the sheer numbers of free sessions I was doing. And I started to notice a trend. The people I spent the least time with were the ones who seemed to be hiring me the most. This was my first clue to what really works!

The next thing that happened was that I reviewed my sales training programs and I noticed how selling was a lot like coaching. I began to see that coaching and selling were like "twin brothers that were separated at birth" so to speak. I began applying my sales skills to my free coaching sessions and discovered something surprising!

I was shocked to find that the people I used my selling skills with got even more value from our free coaching session than the ones where I "coached my heart out". And it didn't matter if they hired me or not they still felt like they got tremendous value from our free session. Then over the years, I kept modifying my approach, refining it, honing it, perfecting it. Finally, I began to share my methods with other coaches and watched them grow their coaching businesses very quickly!

As I mentioned, in my first 6 years, I had only worked with 5 coaches as 1-on-1 clients and 4 out of 5 of them took their businesses to over $100K/year within 18 months. One of them jumped from zero to 6 figures within 90 days and then tripled his income to over $300K/year within the following 12 months.

I've seen a lot of coaches come and go over the years. New coaches on the scene have so much optimism and enthusiasm but that can quickly turn to panic, fear, frustration, and despair when they begin to understand the realities of having their own business.

You have to be able to talk to people about coaching and then have them hire you. But most coaches try to explain coaching in a way that's abstract and has no real compelling meaning to people. That will rarely get you hired.

It can work every now and then just by attracting people through sheer energy and enthusiasm. And that can actually be a bad thing because it can lead you to think that what you're doing actually works. It does work, but not consistently or effectively enough for anyone to make a real living this way.

That's why you've got to have a system that will enroll clients predictably and consistently and that works almost every time. If you don't you could be out of business fast (or struggling for years to get this thing off the ground).

You could be living the dream...

- doing work that's meaningful and fun

- watching clients succeed because of your support

- earning an ever soaring income—$50K, $100K, or even $300K/year!

- enjoying total time, money, and location freedom (when you work with clients over the phone you can coach from anywhere in the world, and you can set your own hours, take time off whenever you want, and enjoy the finer things in life)

Here's what I know about coaches that make $100K per year or more. They all have 1 thing in common. They all use a system for enrolling clients from initial consultations of some sort. Every single one of them.

If you want to earn $100K/year or more as a coach you must have a systematic way of taking someone from "interested" to hiring you on the spot.

Guess what? All coaches that struggle have something in common too. They don't have a systematic way of enrolling clients from free coaching sessions.

Successful coaches are able to save a lot of money to pay for things like their children's education and their retirement because they generate serious revenue and it's all dependent on their ability to enroll clients from their intro session.

On the other hand, people who don't have a system for effectively enrolling clients often worry about money and fear that they are letting down the important people in their lives. They question their decision to get into coaching in the first place and that's extremely dangerous because it can lead to lots of self doubts and sap your confidence.

If you're working lots of hours on your coaching business and most of those hours aren't spent actually working with clients, then let me open your eyes up to something.

There are really only two money making activities in your business. Everything else is a drain on your time.

Money Making Activity #1: Working with clients.

This is pretty obvious because this is what you get paid to do.

Money Making Activity #2: Signing up new clients.

This is where the money really gets made. If you can't GET the clients, you can't coach the clients.

This is also where the hole is in most coach's "money bucket". If you can't sign up new clients consistently, reliably, and for the fees you want to charge, you really can't make the money you want as a coach or help as many people as you'd like to.

What does your track record with free sessions look like? If you've given free coaching sessions to a lot of people, you've probably helped a lot of people with these free coaching sessions. But, if you're like most coaches, you're working your butt off trying to have a really powerful coaching session hoping that the potential client will "see" what a great coach you are and decide to hire you.

Do you sometimes have such a great session that you actually solve whatever challenge they brought up during their free session and they still don't hire you? Or do you have a regular, solid coaching session, but they just don't see the long term impact that ongoing coaching would create?

Either way, you spend 30 minutes or an hour of your time (or even two hours!!), but you walk away with remarks like "I'll think about it". Do you rarely end up getting any clients from all of your efforts?

But you think, "maybe it's not so bad". At first, you figure "I'm getting coaching practice" and keep at it, but eventually you start to wonder:

Is there really a market for coaching?

...Do people ever really pay those fees most coaches seem to be charging?

...Are the only real clients other coaches? Or . . .

...(the worst one) If I can't get clients, I'm not really that good of a coach?

You may have even heard that you shouldn't give away free coaching sessions at all. "The initial session should be a paid session" some people recommend. And maybe you even tried charging for your initial session, but got few takers with that approach (or more likely none) and now you may be about to throw in the towel and give up.

If you're reading this book right now and that has been your story, then I have a special message for you. There is no need to give up! You can really help a lot of people with your coaching & start making crazy good money if you know how to have 'Free Sessions That Sell'.

Have you ever felt "weird" during your free coaching session when it came time to wrap up your free session and start to talk about hiring you and asking them to pay you? I know I have! No one likes to "sell", and more people don't like to be "sold" (although people do love to buy things...especially something that will be of tremendous help to them).

Once I developed this step-by-step system it took away the discomfort. Asking for the money became easy and natural.

When you use the "Free Sessions That Sell" formula, you will feel "rock-solid" about talking to potential clients about how you work, how coaching works, and why they should hire you right now! And, you can get rid of that uncomfortable feeling once and for all!

Here are the main steps of the "Free Sessions That Sell" System. This is how to conduct your introductory sessions in a way that will actually help people "get" how coaching will help them and move them to hire you.

Step 1: Get rapport and connect with your potential clients

Step 2: Find out what your potential clients really, really, *really* want (and it may not be what you think—or even what *they* think).

Step 3: Show them how having what they want will impact their life.

Step 4: Uncover the challenges standing in their way (including the hidden challenges that are sabotaging their success)

Step 5: Show them the impact these challenges are having on their life.

Step 6: Share what you do (in a way that is compelling)

Step 7: Accept Payment . . . (sometimes, they'll want to pay for 6 months in advance. I think you're really going to enjoy it when that happens)

Now you can take these seven key points, and create a script for your free sessions based on this. That will work a lot better than what you might have tried to get clients in the past.

Or if you want you can check out my program, Free Sessions That Sell which includes the tried and true script I've already perfected along with all of the training that teaches the magic phrases, the mindset, the mechanics of a great session, practice buddies, live demos and more.

Check out Free Sessions That Sell here: www.FreeSessionsThatSell.com

CHAPTER 10
Your Next Steps

Thanks for reading this book.

I really hope it gave you a lot of new ideas, inspired you to keep working on building your dream coaching business, and gave you some tools that you can put into practice right away.

If you haven't already, make sure you check out the gift I've included—The Client Getting Email Templates. They are ready for you to use now, so you can get clients today!

And I hope you can avoid the mistake that many people make.

The number one mistake people make with our products and programs is…never studying them and applying the information. I know it sounds crazy. How could someone that just made a financial investment not take the time to use it?

Here's what happens. People are excited. They order the book and then they hope that somehow just by buying it, their business will dramatically change.

Or…they get overwhelmed. They read this book, or hear me on an interview, and they know that I can help them achieve their goals. But they don't know which product or program is the right next step for them and they don't know where to start. And of course they want the biggest results in the shortest time possible!

I don't want either of these things keeping you from getting the results you desire. Let me help with that right now.

I can't make anyone study. But I can help eliminate the overwhelm. You see, I've got three major programs that you can choose to invest in if you want to take everything in this book to the next level.

Each one of these three programs offers a wealth of information on its own. But put them together and you have every piece of the puzzle you need to build a thriving, financially abundant coaching business that allows you to help a ton of people while enjoying the lifestyle you've always wanted.

Here's a bit of information about each one…

#1: Free Sessions That Sell: The Client Sign Up System

This program teaches you how to enroll coaching clients from an initial intro session. You should start here if you are already confident in your coaching and are ready to sign up clients right now.

And if you're in a real hurry, you can skip to session two because the first session teaches an in depth version of free session offer. Since I've already written great free session offers for you, feel free to swipe mine and jump to lesson two.

Get more information on Free Sesssions That Sell here: www.FreeSessionsThatSell.com

#2: Rapid Coaching Academy: The Professional Coach Training System

If you haven't been trained as a coach yet, or if you don't feel certain about the value of your coaching, START HERE.

There are amazing coaching skills, strategies, approaches, and techniques inside this program.

You're going to LOVE it. But…

If you feel ready to start coaching today, or you are already a confident coach, please do not study this program until you've gone through BOTH of the other programs.

Get more information on Rapid Coaching Academy here: www.RapidCoachingAcademy.com

#3: Client Attraction & Money Making Mastery

This program teaches you how to market your coaching so that you have clients chasing you (instead of the other way around).

When you can set yourself up as an expert, infiltrate your target client's secret hang outs, and win over key influencers to start promoting you, you'll have a NEVER-ENDING supply of coaching leads.

Then you'll use "Free Sessions That Sell" to convert those leads into actual, paying clients.

Start out with Free Sessions That Sell and then study this program. There's no sense in doing all the work on your marketing if you can't get enough people to actually hire you. Plus...

Even without a website or business cards or knowing anything about marketing, you can still get paying clients using Free Sessions That Sell.

If you're ready to start coaching people right now and get paid for it, then start with Free Sessions That Sell.

The only time you should start with Client Attraction & Money Making Mastery is if you already have a solid system for signing up clients from intro sessions.

Get more information on Client Attraction & Money Making Mastery here: www.ClientAttractionAndMoneyMakingMastery.com

Remember that it's possible to create a coaching business that you love, that brings you great financial reward and the lifestyle you choose, all while making a difference for a whole lot of people.

And know that I'm here to help you - if you want my help. I've been through the journey of starting a coaching business from scratch, and I've tried pretty much everything possible to figure out what works the best and what doesn't.

I've built a multi-million dollar coaching business myself, and over the last decade I've also helped thousands of other coaches achieve the results they want for their businesses.

Along the way I've seen far too many good coaches struggling to build their businesses and get clients. I want to change the game for you, and I hope you take the information and strategies in this book and put them into practice.

Let me know how it goes, and how I can help.

People need our help. Let's get people coached!

FREE GIFT
"Client-Getting" Email Templates

Choose the "Client-Getting Email" that matches your target market (then copy it, paste it into an email, and send it out)

Here is a list of all the target markets—choose which one is best for you and use these pre-written emails to get clients today!

1. No Niche Market Yet, Use This Email To Get Clients

2. Small Business Owners

3. Sales Professionals

4. Leaders/Executives

5. Career Coach

6. Weight Loss Coaching

7. Coach For Single Women

8. Coach For Single Men

9. Relationship Coach For Couples

10. Parenting Coach

11. "Other" (The Target Market Isn't Listed Here)

And be sure to check out the Bonus Article: **"7 Secrets To Keep Clients From Slipping Through Your Fingers"**

If You Don't Have a Niche Market, Send This Email:

Subject Line: Secrets of Achievement & Change (Special Inside)...

Hi FIRST NAME,

Do you have something you want to change or achieve in your life? Maybe you'd like to...

=> start a business

=> find new love

=> get a new career (or a raise)

=> lose weight

=> get your child(ren) to behave better

=> or something else

No matter what you'd like to change or achieve, the secrets to success are the same...

#1: Get clear. As specifically as possible, decide what you want. The more clear you are on what you want to have in your life, the more likely you are to achieve it.

#2: Get perspective. Most people don't tell anyone what they want or what they are struggling with and because of that they don't get an outside perspective.

#3: Get support. Very few people (if any) achieve anything great alone. Sports stars have teammates and coaches

Be willing to ask the people in your life to support you.

** Special ZERO COST "Rapid Change" Coaching Session **

Do you have something SPECIAL, something important for you to change? If you want to speed up your success rate, then I'd like to help you do it with a special 1-on-1 personal "Rapid Change" coaching session where we'll work together to...

=> Create a crystal clear vision for "ultimate success" so you know exactly what you want, where you're headed, and what you need to do to make it happen.

=> Uncover hidden challenges that may be sabotaging your ability to make changes that last or that are slowing down your progress

=> Leave this session renewed, re-energized, and inspired to finally achieve the change you seek- once and for all

If you'd like to take advantage of this very special, very limited, and totally FREE 30 minute "Rapid Change" coaching session, click reply and answer these questions...

1. What do you most want to change today?

2. Have you tried to change this before?

3. What have you attempted in the past that didn't work?

4. Why do you think it didn't work?

5. On a scale of 0-10, how important is it for you to achieve change today?

6. What other areas of your life do you want to change (if any)?

7. Full Name

8. Email Address

9. Phone #

10. Time Zone

Check off the areas you'd most like to work on...

__ Business

__ Weight Loss

__ Relationship (get into one)

__ Relationship (improve the one I'm in)

__ Career Change

__ Parenting Challenges

__ Other

Since we're making this offer for the first time right now and we don't know how intense the response will be, we can't guarantee a coaching session for everyone.

We'll take as many people as we can and then start a waiting list. You can expect to get contacted by our team to schedule your session within the next 3 business days.

If you don't hear from us, it means we've received more requests than we can handle right now and if something opens up we'll get in touch with you at a later time.

Again, to take advantage of this offer, simply click reply and answer the questions listed above.

Warmest Regards,

[Your name here]

PS: The sooner you send us your answers, the more likely you are to get a session. Click reply now.

Get Small Business Owners As Your Clients With This Email:

Subject Line: Get the Business Breakthrough You Need...

Hi FIRST NAME,

If you've been working to grow your business for a while now and things aren't happening as fast as you want, then I'd like to help you create a MAJOR business BREAKTHROUGH. Here's the scoop...

I've heard from a lot of small businesses that are having an especially difficult time getting their business to grow fast these days. After hearing about so many people's struggles, I decided to do something about it...

** NEW, For a Limited Time **

I'd like to invite you to take advantage of a special, "Business Breakthrough" coaching session where we'll work together to...

=> Create a crystal clear vision for your "ultimate business success" and the "perfect lifestyle" you'd like your business to provide

=> Uncover hidden challenges that may be sabotaging the growth of your business and keeping you working too many hours

=> Leave this session renewed, re-energized, and inspired to turn your business into a highly profitable, revenue-generating machine that practically runs itself...

If you'd like to take advantage of this very special, very limited, and totally FREE 30 minute "Business Breakthrough" coaching session, click reply and answer these questions...

1. How long have you had your business?

2. What kind of product/service do you provide?

3. What are your revenue goals for the next 12 months?

4. What was your business revenue over the last 12 months?

(ballpark)

5. What do you see as the major challenges holding you and your business back from growing at the pace you want?

6. On a scale of 0-10, how important is it for you to overcome your challenges and achieve your goals today?

7. Full Name

8. Email Address

9. Phone #

10. Time Zone

Check off the areas you'd most like to work on…

__ Marketing

__ Sales Process

__ Turning Your Team Into High Performers

__ Cash Flow Strategies

__ Customer Service

__ Systemizing & Streamlining Processes

__ Leadership & Delegation

__ Other

Since we're making this offer for the first time right now and we don't know how intense the response will be, we can't guarantee a coaching session for everyone.

We'll take as many people as we can and then start a waiting list. You can expect to get contacted by our team to schedule your session within the next 3 business days.

If you don't hear from us, it means we've received more requests than we can handle right now and if something opens up we'll get in touch with you at a later time.

Again, to take advantage of this offer, simply click reply and answer the questions listed above.

Warmest Regards,

[Your name here]

PS: The sooner you send us your answers, the more likely you are to get a session. Click reply now.

Get Sales Professionals As Your Clients With This Email:

Subject: Get the Sales Breakthrough You Need...

Dear FIRST NAME,

If you've been struggling to close enough sales and you'd like a major breakthrough, then I'd like to invite you to take advantage of a special, "Sky-Rocket Your Sales" personal, 1-on-1 coaching session where we will work together to...

=> Create a crystal clear vision for the sales success you desire (we'll set targets for prospecting activities, and „close ratios" that will give you the lifestyle you desire)

=> Uncover hidden challenges that may be sabotaging your sales success (we'll pinpoint specific areas that cause breakdowns in the sales process so you can make immediate changes)

=> Leave this session renewed, re-energized, and inspired to break your personal sales records and enjoy a great income.

If you'd like to take advantage of this very special, very limited, and totally FREE 30 minute "Sky-Rocket Your Sales" coaching session, click reply and answer the questions below...

1. How long have you had your current sales position?

2. What kind of product/service do you sell?

3. What are your sales commission goals for the next 12 months?

4. What were your sales commissions from the last 12 months? (ballpark)

5. What do you see as the major challenges holding you back from selling as much as you want?

6. On a scale of 0-10, how important is it for you to overcome your challenges and achieve your sales and lifestyle goals today?

7. Full Name

8. Email Address

9. Phone #

10. Time Zone

Check off the areas you'd like to work on…

__ Finding a Great Prospect List

__ Prospecting

__ Assessing Needs

__ Presenting Your Offer

__ Overcoming Objections

__ Closing the Sale

__ Getting Referrals & Up-Selling

__ Other

Since we're making this offer for the first time right now and we don't know how intense the response will be, we can't guarantee a coaching session for everyone.

We'll take as many people as we can and then start a waiting list. You can expect to get contacted by our team to schedule your session within the next 3 business days.

If you don't hear from us, it means we've received more requests than we can handle right now and if something opens up we'll get in touch with you at a later time.

Again, to take advantage of this offer, simply click reply and answer the questions listed above.

Warmest Regards,

[Your name here]

PS: The sooner you send us your answers, the more likely you are to get a session. Click reply now.

Get Leaders & Executives As Your Clients With This Email:

Subject: The secret to getting more from your team…

Hey FIRST NAME,

If you want to get more out of your team for any of these reasons:

=> Because the number of people on your team has been reduced and yet you're expected to produce the same or better results

=> Your team is not producing the results that are expected from you and your team and you're concerned that your bosses and/or superiors and peers are not going to be happy about that

=> Members of your team are undermining each other or worse undermining you, causing conflicts and frustrations for you and you'd like to turn your team in to a well oiled machine...

Then, I'd like to help you squeeze the most out of your team as possible by offering you a special one-on-one "Modern Leadership Mastery Coaching Session".

During this session we will…

=> Create a crystal clear vision for the results that you want your team to produce, for the way that you'd like your team to interact with each other and for the kind of people you would like to have on your team

=> Uncover hidden challenges that may be sabotaging your success with leadership and team building

=> You'll leave the session renewed, reenergized and inspired to create a powerful results-driven team that gets things done so that you can be the office hero and still have a flourishing personal life

To claim this special coaching session simply click reply and answer the following questions:

1. How long have you been in this leadership position?

2. What are the biggest leadership challenges you're facing today?

3. On a scale of zero to 10 how important is it to you to get better results from your team?

4. What are your ultimate aspirations and goals as a leader?

Be sure to also include your name, phone number and email address when you reply so that someone from our office can get back to you and schedule your session within the next 24 to 48 hours.

All the best.

Yours truly,

[Your name here]

PS: The sooner you send us your answers, the more likely you are to get a session. Click reply now.

If You're a Career Coach, Send This Email:

Subject: Here's how to stand out from all other job seekers…

Hey FIRST NAME,

If you've been struggling to get interviews and land a great job fast, then I'd like to invite you to take advantage of a special, "Get Hired Now" personal, 1-on-1 coaching session where we will work together to…

=> Create a crystal clear vision for the type of job you want, the income level you desire, and what it will take to make it happen—FAST

=> Uncover hidden challenges that may be sabotaging your success with getting interviews and ace-ing them

=> Leave this session renewed, re-energized, and inspired to get hired now in the best, highest paying job you've ever had.

If you'd like to take advantage of this very special, very limited, and totally FREE 30 minute "Get Hired Now" coaching session, hit reply and answer the following questions:

1. How long have you been unemployed?

2. What was the last job you had?

3. Did you like it?

4. How long did you have that job?

5. What were you paid at that job?

6. On a scale of 0-10, how important is it for you to find a job right now?

7. Full Name

8. Email Address

9. Phone #

10. Time Zone

Since we're making this offer for the first time right now and we don't know how intense the response will be, we can't guarantee a coaching session for everyone. We'll take as many people as we can and then start a waiting list.

You can expect to get contacted by our team to schedule your session within the next 3 business days. If you don't hear from us, it means we've received more requests than we can handle right now and if something opens up we'll get in touch with you at a later time.

Yours truly,

[Your name here]

PS: The sooner you send us your answers, the more likely you are to get a session. Click reply now.

If You Want Weight Loss Coaching Clients, Use This Email:

Subject: How THIN do you **REALLY** want to get?

Hey FIRST NAME,

If you could push a button and get all the way down to the weight you know deep down you'd REALLY like to be at, what would you weigh?

Most people "lie" to themselves when they think about how much weight they'd like to lose. They say 'I'd like to lose 15 or 20 pounds". But, when we get 60 pounds over-weight or more, 20 pounds is barely noticeable (which is one of the reasons why we tend to keep gaining weight -adding another 5 pounds is hard to notice). BUT...

If you'd like to finally get ALLLLLL the way down to your sexiest, most confident weight - once and for all AND...

If you'd like to get my personal support to make it happen, then check this out...

For a limited time I'm offering a special "Finally Thin Forever" Coaching Session (a $350 value) for ZERO COST.

During this powerful, 1-on-1 coaching session, we'll work together to...

=> Create a crystal clear vision for the ideal life you'll be living in your new, slim, sexy, & confident body

=> Uncover hidden challenges that may be sabotaging your weight loss efforts and keeping you fat

=> Leave this session renewed, inspired, and ready to finally lose all of the weight you want- once and for all.

To claim your special "Finally Thin Forever "coaching session today, simply click reply and answer these questions:

1. How long have you been struggling to lose weight?

2. On a scale of zero to 10 how important is it for you to lose weight and keep it off once and for all?

3. What have you tried doing to lose weight in the past?

4. What happened with those approaches?

5. What do you see as your biggest challenge with weight loss?

Be sure to include your name, phone number and email address so someone from our office can get back to you within the next 24 to 48 hours to schedule your one-on-one "Finally Thin Forever."

(Please allow up to 60 minutes for this coaching session.)

Click reply now to claim your session today.

Warmest regards,

[Your name here]

PS: The sooner you send us your answers, the more likely you are to get a session. Click reply now.

Get Single Women that Want Love As Your Clients With This Email:

Subject: Find Mr. Right Today...

Hey FIRST NAME,

If you'd like to find Mr. Right today and you'd like to have that experience of your Prince Charming, whatever that may be for you -- tall dark and handsome, powerful, attractive, sexy, whatever kind of man you would really love in your heart of hearts to have in your life. To be able to enjoy the kind of relationship that you're looking for where you go out to movies and go on vacations together and go out to dinner with your couple friends and all those great couple experiences...

Maybe you'll even want to get married and have a family...

It all starts with finding the right guy, finding your Mr. Right and I'd like to help you do that.

For a limited time I am offering a special "Find Mr. Right Coaching Session" for ZERO COST.

During this special 1-on-1 coaching session we'll work together to...

=> Create a crystal clear vision for the kind of man that you'd like to attract and the kind of relationship that you'd like to have

=> We'll uncover hidden challenges that may be sabotaging your success with men and dating

=> You'll leave the session renewed, reenergized and inspired to find and keep a great man once and for all

To claim your special "Find Mr. Right Coaching Session" today, simply click reply and answer these questions:

1. How long have you been single?

2. On a scale of zero to 10 how important is it for you to get in to a relationship now?

3. What do you see as your biggest relationship challenges?

4. What would you most like help with when it comes to men and dating?

Be sure to include your name, phone number and email address so someone from our office can get back to you within the next 24 to 48 hours to schedule your one-on-one "Find Mr. Right Coaching Session."

Click reply now to claim your session today. Until next time...

Yours truly,

[Your name here]

P.S. I can't wait to hear how great things are for you once you've got that great man in your life!

Get Single Men To Hire You Who Want Dates/Love With This Email:

Subject: Get the girl tonight…

Hey FIRST NAME,

We've all been stopped short when it comes to getting a date with an attractive woman.

If you've ever seen a girl on the street and you've thought, "Man I'd really like to talk to her," or at a restaurant or at a club or something like that but yet you didn't follow through, you didn't go up and ask her out, you didn't go up and get a phone number from her…

If you've ever found yourself stopped short when it comes to dating the attractive woman that you would like to date I would like to help you out. And, if you've ever had the courage to go up and ask out an attractive woman and it just didn't work out I'd like to help you as well.

See, when it comes to dating women there is a right way and a wrong way to go about having the kind of success that you're looking for and I'd like to personally help you become the kind of man that can naturally and easily approach extremely attractive woman, carry on fun conversations with them, easily get their phone numbers, feel very comfortable asking them out on dates and ultimately having the kind of relationship with women that you really want.

In order to help you out I've decided to have a personal one-on-one session with as many of my readers and subscribers as I can over the next couple of weeks.

I probably won't be able to work with everybody but the sooner you request this session the more likely you are to be able to get on my schedule. This coaching session is called the "Confidence with Women Coaching Session".

During the "Confidence with Women Coaching Session" we will work together to…

=> Create a crystal clear vision for the kind of woman that you'd like to have in your life and the kind of relationship you'd like to have with her

=> We'll uncover hidden challenges that may be sabotaging your success with women and dating.

=> You'll leave the session renewed, reenergized and inspired to take consistent action in your dating and love life so that you can finally have the success with women that you've always wanted.

To get your "Confidence with Women Coaching Session" today, simply click reply to this email and answer the following questions:

1. How long have you been single?

2. On a scale of zero to 10 how important is it for you to get this area of your life called relationship handled once and for all?

3. What do you see as your biggest challenges with women and dating?

4. What was your greatest relationship success to date?

Click reply and be sure to include your name and phone number so that someone from our office can give you a call and get you scheduled for this special 30 minute "Confidence with Women Coaching Session" today.

Until next time...

Yours truly,

[Your name here]

PS: The sooner you send us your answers, the more likely you are to get a session. Click reply now.

If You're a Relationship Coach, Get Couples As Your Clients:

Subject: Save your relationship…

Hey FIRST NAME,

Is your relationship on the rocks? Are you worried that your relationship may not last much longer? Have you been thinking about ending the relationship yourself or are you worried that your partner is going to end the relationship sometime soon?

If so, my heart goes out to you. We've all been in these kinds of situations at some point in our lives and they are never easy. In fact, relationships are often times our greatest source of happiness and can be our greatest source of despair.

Therefore, for a limited time I've decided to offer a special one-on-one "Relationship Rescue Coaching Session". During this session we'll work together to…

=> Create a crystal clear vision for the kind of happy relationship you'd like to have

=> Uncover hidden challenges that may be sabotaging your relationship success

=> You'll leave this session renewed, reenergized and inspired to turn your current relationship into the relationship of your dreams (or know if it's time to get out)

To claim your 30 minute "Relationship Rescue Coaching Session" simply click reply and answer the following questions:

1. How long have you been in this relationship?

2. On a scale of zero to 10 how important is it for you to save this relationship?

3. What are the three biggest challenges you are facing in your relationship?

Be sure to include your name, email address and phone number when you request your session so that we can get in touch with you to schedule your session.

Warmest regards,

[Your name here]

PS: The sooner you send us your answers, the more likely you are to get a session. Click reply now.

If You're a Parenting Coach, Use This Email to Get Clients:

Subject: I'll help you turn your child's BAD behavior around...

Hey FIRST NAME,

Would you like my help turning your child's bad behavior around? If you have tried everything and haven't been able to completely get the respect and great behavior from your child that you deserve and you'd like to turn this around once and for all then I'd like to help you do it.

For a limited time, I'm offering a special zero cost "Demons to Angels Coaching Session".

During this powerful 30 minute coaching session we'll work together to...

=> Create a crystal clear vision for the kind of behavior and the kind of relationship that you'd like to have with your child or children.

=> Uncover hidden challenges that may be sabotaging your ability to get the respect and good behavior from your child or children that you deserve.

=> You'll leave the session renewed, reenergized and inspired to parent your children into the happy, healthy, successful, respectful and fun children that are at their core once and for all.

To claim your "Demons to Angels Coaching Session", simply click reply and answer the following questions:

1. How many children do you have?

2. How many of these children are causing problems in your home?

3. On a scale of zero to 10 how important is it to get your child's behavior turned around once and for all?

4. What are behavior challenges that are causing the most frustrations for you as a parent?

5. What have you tried to turn your child's behavior around in the past and how did that work out for you?

To claim one of these special zero cost coaching sessions click reply now and answer the questions above. Be sure to also include your name, phone number and email address so we can get in touch with you to schedule your coaching session right away.

All the best,

[Your name here]

PS: The sooner you send us your answers, the more likely you are to get a session. Click reply now.

OTHER/ "The People I Coach Aren't Listed Here... What Should I Do?"

If you coach people in an area that isn't covered here, please send me an email to Christian@CoachesWithClients.com and tell me what you coach people on. If I hear from enough coaches with the same kind of thing, I'll write one for you.

In the meantime, see if you can take one of the ones listed above and change it to match your own personal target market.

For example, if you're a Real Estate coach, maybe you can use the "sales professionals" email and insert words like "Realtor" and "transactions", etc. If you can't see a way to use one of the free sessions above AND we don't get enough requests for a session based on what you coach, that could mean you need more work on your target market. It might be too far "out there" or you just might not be looking at what the "market wants".

A lot of coaches focus on what they (the coach) wants to help people with instead of looking at the marketplace and seeing what people are actually looking for help with. If you've been struggling with your niche market, rest assured, we can help.

BONUS CHAPTER

"7 Secrets to Stop Clients from Slipping through Your Fingers..."

#1) ACT FAST. When people reply to your "Client Getting Email" and say "Yes, I want to have a coaching session with you", you can't wait a week to get back to them. Why? People will forget what the whole thing is about. I recommend getting back to people the very next day after they send in their request. This way you don't seem too eager or wait too long so that people forget about you.

#2) USE THE PHONE. Actually call people to schedule your sessions. Emails get lost or put off very easily. Pick up the phone and call people to set up the session. If you get voicemail, let them know you've sent them an email and they need to follow the steps in that email.

Example Follow Up Email...

Hi NAME,

I just left you a voicemail in response to your request for the free (IN-SERT NAME of the SESSION) coaching session where we'll work on (INSERT TOPIC they said they wanted to work on with you).

You can call me back at XXX-YYY-ZZZZ or you can schedule the session yourself here (Insert link to your online calendar).

Warmest Regards,

YOUR NAME

#3) GET HELP. If you can, have someone else make the phone calls (your assistant, brother, sister, husband, wife, etc.) on your behalf. It makes you look more professional. However, I've made the calls myself in the past and if you can't get anyone to help you, don't sweat it.

#4) LIMIT YOUR AVAILABILITY. You might want to use www. TimeDriver.com so that people can schedule themselves. However, limit your availability. You don't want to show people that there is very limited demand for you by showing them a billion free spots on your schedule.

You can always add additional availability as things fill up. Also, it's a great idea to schedule your sessions an hour apart, but not to have them all over the place in your schedule. Bunch them together (but not too close). This way you'll be "in the zone" as you're doing your sessions.

#5) Temper Your Expectations. This strategy has worked OVER and OVER, thousands of times for myself and other coaches that I've shared this with. You might get just 1 person that wants to have a session with you, or 500. Personally, I have found that the number of people that sign up for these sessions is about the same as the number of people that sign up for a free tele-class that you might offer. Any results you get should be an improvement over waiting around for people to call you up and tell you they want to hire you.

#6) REPEAT - Use Follow Up Emails To Get More Clients. Send this email 3 times to get the best results.

The second time you send it (perhaps 48 hours later), you can simply add this to the "Client Getting Email" (from above)...

2nd Email Subject Line: Did you see this?

2nd Email: (add this above the body of the "client getting email") Did you see this? I sent it out a couple of days ago and I wanted to make sure you didn't miss out.

For Email # 3 Send this out on the 5th day after the original email 3 days after email #2...

Final Email Subject Line: Last Chance to Work With Me To (INSERT RESULT HERE)...

Final Email: (add this above the body of the "client getting email") Last chance to claim your special 1-on-1 coaching sessions with me. See details below...

#7) TAKE ACTION. Copy the "Client Getting Email" that most closely matches your target market from the list above and paste it into an email and send it out. You can't get results without action. Do it now. Then email me in a week or so and let me know how it went.

ABOUT THE AUTHOR

Christian Mickelsen is a leading authority on personal development and personal coaching. He's the author of *How to Quickly Get Started As a Personal Coach: Make Great Money Changing People's Lives*, *Get Clients Today: How To Get A Surge Of New, High Paying Coaching Clients Today And Every Day*, and the upcoming book *The Solution To All Of Life's Problems*.

He's been seen in Forbes, Yahoo Finance, MSN, and the Boston Globe.

He's the founder of IMPACT - the world's leading association for personal coaches

As a personal coach for over 13 years and a trainer of coaches, he's helped countless thousands around the world experience the life changing power of coaching. He's on a mission to get the whole world coached.

He lives in San Diego, California with his wife and two daughters.

Find him here:

http://www.CoachesWithClients.com

http://www.ImpactForCoaches.org

http://www.ChristianMickelsen.com

http://www.facebook.com/christian.mickelsen

http://coacheswithclients.com/twitter

http://coacheswithclients.com/facebook

http://coacheswithclients.com/linkedin

Or contact him at Coaches With Clients:

Christian@CoachesWithClients.com

619-320-8185